FROM:

GREAT MINDS DRINK ALIKE

Written and compiled by
VIRGINIA REYNOLDS

Illustrated by
KERI BARBAS STECKLER

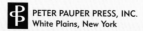

PETER PAUPER PRESS, INC.
White Plains, New York

For Mady,

my partner in wine

Illustrations © Keri Barbas Steckler
Designed by Heather Zschock

Copyright © 2010
Peter Pauper Press, Inc.
202 Mamaroneck Avenue
White Plains, NY 10601
ISBN 978-1-4413-0336-3
Printed in China
7 6 5 4 3 2 1

Visit us at www.peterpauper.com

GREAT MINDS
DRINK ALIKE

• INTRODUCTION •

I't's said that "In wine, there is truth." In wine, and beer, and especially in martinis, there is also wit and wisdom. As far back as ancient Greece, great minds extolled the virtues of the fruits of the vine with humor, and happily shared the inspiration drawn from knocking back a glass or two. We invite you to raise your glass and toast the

great literary minds of history—
from Aristophanes to Frank Zappa—
who could smooth away life's rough
edges with a bon mot and a belt
of booze.

Remember, life is
too short to drink bad
wine. Cheers!

ONE TEQUILA, TWO TEQUILA, THREE TEQUILA, FLOOR.

George Carlin

Always carry a corkscrew and the wine shall provide itself.

Basil Bunting

BEER IS PROOF THAT GOD LOVES US AND WANTS US TO BE HAPPY.

Benjamin Franklin

I have taken more out of alcohol than alcohol has taken out of me.

WINSTON CHURCHILL

WORK IS THE CURSE OF THE DRINKING CLASSES.

Oscar Wilde

The secret to a long life
is to stay busy, get
plenty of exercise and
don't drink too much.
Then again,
don't drink too little.

HERMAN SMITH-JOHANNSEN

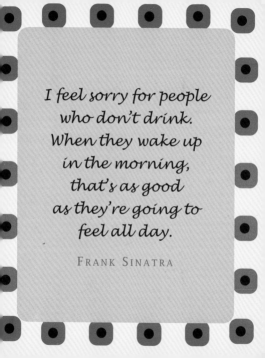

I feel sorry for people who don't drink. When they wake up in the morning, that's as good as they're going to feel all day.

FRANK SINATRA

WHY DON'T YOU GET OUT OF THAT WET COAT AND INTO A DRY MARTINI?

Robert Benchley to Ginger Rogers,
in The Major and the Minor

A woman drove me
to drink and I didn't
even have the decency
to thank her.

W. C. FIELDS

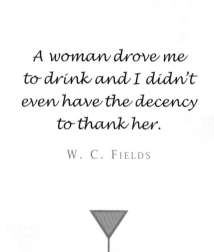

Martinis should always be stirred, not shaken, so that the molecules lie sensuously one on top of the other.

W. SOMERSET MAUGHAM

It takes only one drink to get me drunk. The trouble is, I can't remember if it's the thirteenth or the fourteenth.

GEORGE BURNS

ONE MORE DRINK,
AND I'LL BE UNDER
THE HOST.

Dorothy Parker

I DRINK TO MAKE OTHER PEOPLE INTERESTING.

George Jean Nathan

If you were to ask me if I'd ever had the bad luck to miss my daily cocktail, I'd have to say that I doubt it; where certain things are concerned, I plan ahead.

LUIS BUÑUEL

FOR HER FIFTH WEDDING, THE BRIDE WORE BLACK AND CARRIED A SCOTCH AND SODA.

Phyllis Battelle

I AM NOT A HEAVY DRINKER. I CAN SOMETIMES GO FOR HOURS WITHOUT TOUCHING A DROP.

Noel Coward

I hate to advocate drugs, alcohol, violence, or insanity to anyone, but they've always worked for me.

Hunter S. Thompson

*Why don't Jews drink?
It interferes with
their suffering.*

HENNY YOUNGMAN

Let there be dancing
in the streets, drinking
in the saloons, and
necking in the parlor!

Groucho Marx,
in A Night at the Opera

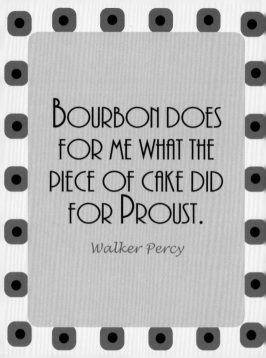

BOURBON DOES FOR ME WHAT THE PIECE OF CAKE DID FOR PROUST.

Walker Percy

There comes a time
in every woman's
life when the only
thing that helps is a
glass of champagne.

Bette Davis,
in Old Acquaintance

Sorrow can be alleviated by good sleep, a bath, and a glass of wine.

Saint Thomas Aquinas

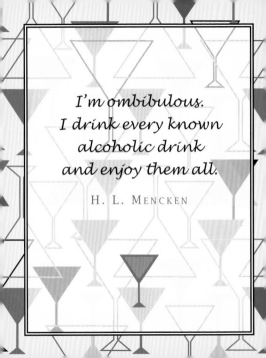

I'm ombibulous.
I drink every known
alcoholic drink
and enjoy them all.

H. L. MENCKEN

Tequila is Mexico.
It's the only product
that identifies us
as a culture.

CARMELITA ROMAN

I believe that if life gives you lemons, you should make lemonade .... And try to find somebody whose life has given them vodka, and have a party.

RON WHITE

You can't be a real country unless you have a beer and an airline. It helps if you have some kind of football team, or some nuclear weapons, but at the very least you need a beer.

FRANK ZAPPA

The relationship between a Russian and a bottle of vodka is almost mystical.

RICHARD OWEN

HERE'S CHAMPAGNE TO OUR REAL FRIENDS, AND REAL PAIN TO OUR SHAM FRIENDS!

Author unknown

I THINK I HAD IT IN THE
BACK OF MY MIND
THAT I WANTED TO
SOUND LIKE A
DRY MARTINI.

Paul Desmond,
of the Dave Brubeck Quartet, when
asked about the sound of his sax

*Without question,
the greatest invention
in the history of mankind
is beer. Oh, I grant you
that the wheel was
also a fine invention,
but the wheel does not
go nearly as well
with pizza.*

DAVE BARRY

BE WARY OF STRONG
DRINK. IT CAN MAKE
YOU SHOOT AT TAX
COLLECTORS...
AND MISS.

Robert A. Heinlein

I CAN'T DIE UNTIL THE GOVERNMENT FINDS A SAFE PLACE TO BURY MY LIVER.

Phil Harris

You're not drunk if you can lie on the floor without holding on.

DEAN MARTIN

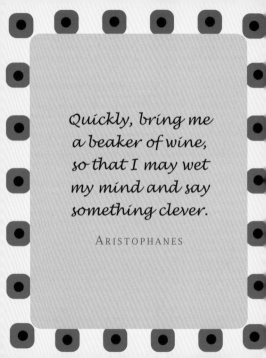

Quickly, bring me
a beaker of wine,
so that I may wet
my mind and say
something clever.

ARISTOPHANES

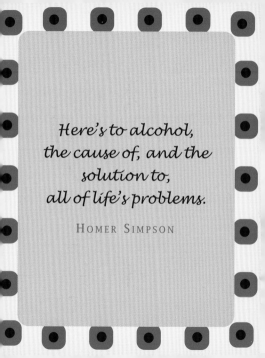

Here's to alcohol,
the cause of, and the
solution to,
all of life's problems.

HOMER SIMPSON

I DISTRUST CAMELS,
AND ANYONE ELSE
WHO CAN GO A WEEK
WITHOUT A DRINK.

Joe E. Lewis

I am prepared to believe that a dry martini slightly impairs the palate, but think what it does for the soul.

ALEC WAUGH

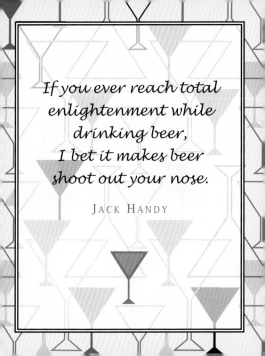

*If you ever reach total
enlightenment while
drinking beer,
I bet it makes beer
shoot out your nose.*

JACK HANDY

*Sure I eat what I advertise.
Sure I eat Wheaties for
breakfast. A good bowl of
Wheaties with bourbon for
breakfast can't be beat.*

DIZZY DEAN

I ENVY PEOPLE WHO DRINK—AT LEAST THEY KNOW WHAT TO BLAME EVERYTHING ON.

Oscar Levant

Now tequila may be the favored beverage of outlaws. But that doesn't mean it gives them preferential treatment.

Tom Robbins

NEVER ACCEPT A DRINK FROM A UROLOGIST.

Erma Bombeck

I DRINK TOO MUCH.
THE LAST TIME I GAVE
A URINE SAMPLE IT HAD
AN OLIVE IN IT.

Joe E. Lewis

GIN AND WATER IS THE SOURCE OF ALL MY INSPIRATION.

Lord Byron

When you stop
drinking, you have
to deal with this
marvelous personality
that started you
drinking in the
first place.

JIMMY BRESLIN

I DRINK NO MORE THAN A SPONGE.

François Rabelais

BEAUTY IS IN THE
EYE OF THE BEER
HOLDER.

Kinky Friedman

THE BEST USE OF BAD WINE IS TO DRIVE AWAY POOR RELATIONS.

French proverb

Something about glamour interested me. All my schoolbooks had drawings of women on terraces with a cocktail and a cigarette.

BILL BLASS

The proper union of gin and vermouth is a great and sudden glory; it is one of the happiest marriages on earth, and one of the shortest lived.

BERNARD DeVOTO

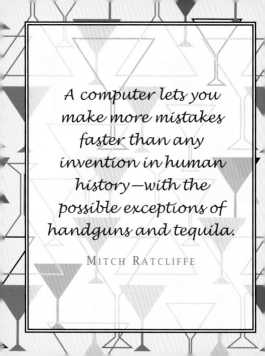

A computer lets you make more mistakes faster than any invention in human history—with the possible exceptions of handguns and tequila.

MITCH RATCLIFFE

The three-martini lunch is the epitome of American efficiency. Where else can you get an earful, a bellyful, and a snootful at the same time?

GERALD FORD

The proper behavior all through the holiday season is to be drunk. This drunkenness culminates on New Year's Eve, when you get so drunk you kiss the person you're married to.

P. J. O'ROURKE

My rule of life prescribed as an absolutely sacred rite smoking cigars and also the drinking of alcohol before, after, and if need be, during all meals and in the intervals between them.

WINSTON CHURCHILL

A meal without wine is like a day without sunshine, except that on a day without sunshine you can still get drunk.

LEE ENTREKIN

LET'S ALL DRINK GIN AND MAKE WRY FACES.

Bob Hope

WINE IS BOTTLED POETRY.

Robert Louis Stevenson

GREAT LOVE AFFAIRS START WITH CHAMPAGNE AND END WITH TISANE.

Honoré de Balzac

The only way that I could figure they could improve upon Coca-Cola, one of life's most delightful elixirs, which studies prove will heal the sick and occasionally raise the dead, is to put rum or bourbon in it.

LEWIS GRIZZARD

Do not allow children to mix drinks. It is unseemly and they use too much vermouth.

Fran Lebowitz

If the Lord hadn't intended us to have a three-martini lunch, then why do you suppose he put all those olive trees in the Holy Land?

JIM WRIGHT

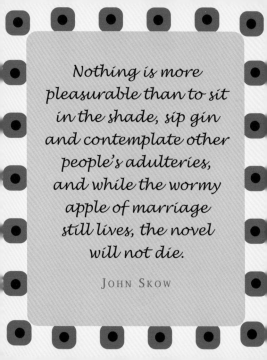

Nothing is more pleasurable than to sit in the shade, sip gin and contemplate other people's adulteries, and while the wormy apple of marriage still lives, the novel will not die.

JOHN SKOW

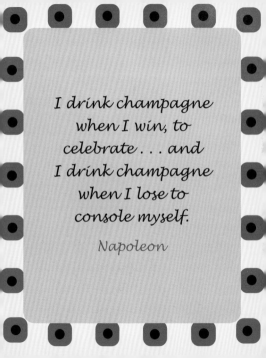

I drink champagne when I win, to celebrate . . . and I drink champagne when I lose to console myself.

Napoleon

HAPPINESS IS FINDING TWO OLIVES IN YOUR MARTINI WHEN YOU'RE HUNGRY.

Johnny Carson

As long as you represent me as represent me as praising alcohol I shall not complain.

H. L. Mencken